POPE FRANCIS
Embrace of Hope
COMPASSION IN TIMES OF ILLNESS

Italian Text Edited by
Edmondo A. Caruana and Lorenzo Tagliaferri

Libreria Editrice

United States Conference of (

Washington, DC

First Printing, April 2018

ISBN 978-1-60137-584-1
ISBN (CHA Version) 978-1-60137-601-5

INTRODUCTION

Pope Francis lives his Petrine ministry close to the faithful. This is particularly clear with regards to those who, for one reason or another, live on the margins, such as the sick, who hold a special place in the Argentinian pope's preaching.

This work is a collection of Pope Francis's most significant words to the sick. It is a series of valuable reflections, considerations, and prayers taken from his speeches, messages, homilies, and *Angeluses* over a period of about four years, from his election to the See of Peter to June 2017. Thanks to the pope's spontaneity, his attention to the weakest, and his simple yet effective language, his careful consideration for the sick leaves an impression on the hearts of people and acts as a balm and a sign of hope that opens the hearts of readers to the fervent love of God the Father.

Pope Francis's words emphasize the importance of the person who, despite suffering from serious illness, maintains his or her inestimable value and forever remains worthy and valuable in the eyes of God and the Church. The sick person should not, therefore, feel like he or she is a burden or an obstacle for others, nor should he or she feel the need to run away or hide, out of shame or fear of becoming a kind of constraint or encumbrance for family members, friends, and relatives. The sick person is indeed a spiritual resource, an authentic asset to every Christian community and to the Church as a whole into whose life he or she is fully integrated. "The world of illness is a world of pain. Sick people suffer, they reflect the suffering Christ: there is no need to fear drawing near to Christ who is suffering" (Speech, March 21, 2015). The sick are indeed the flesh of Christ, indispensable, because they manifest the memory and wisdom of life, which is to be handed down to others (often bringing peace to those who visit them), and because they are full participants in the Church's mission.

Unfortunately, the "culture of waste" mentality that is becoming all too common in today's society affects the sick as well. With his exhortations, the pope, who has always been aware of this kind of culture, of authentic practical atheism, aims to ensure that a radical and hoped for change of direction can occur, by pointing to the Church as the faithful teacher to be followed, for her total commitment and absolute closeness to those who suffer and feel marginalized.

It is a concise collection of great emotional intensity that breaks ideological and cultural prejudices toward the sick. The collection turns suffering into an important school of life to help humanity understand how closeness in illness and experiences of ecclesial fraternity are fundamental in helping families through complicated situations of pain and suffering.

These contexts help us understand what the Kingdom of God is, and according to Pope Francis, they are the Lord's authentic gestures of love.

By opening oneself up to awareness of illness, one solidifies and strengthens his or her family relationships, enriches his or her heart, and learns to confront suffering and the experience of limitations.

The sick person is always a creature of God. He or she does not become a mere object, and the individual definitely does not lose his or her value. "In the first place there is the inviolable dignity of every human being from the moment of conception until the final breath" (Speech, October 2, 2017; see also Message for the 2017 World Day of the Sick, December 8, 2016).

The Holy Father has fought since the beginning of his papacy to oppose the "culture of waste" (which has painful consequences, especially in the healthcare sector) and to promote a culture of encounter with the sick, so as to overcome the limitations and divisions of the experience of illness and suffering. Each person has dignity, and so, as the pope reiterates, each individual must have equal access to medical care, regardless of socio-economic, geographical, or cultural factors. In the healthcare sector, therefore, it is essential to optimize the resources that are available to preserve human life. For this to be avoided, resources must be used in an ethical and responsible manner, so as to not penalize the weakest. The sick, whose health is greatly compromised, must therefore be treated with regard, like any other patient.

Therefore, it is important to plan and implement operational strategies and obtain the necessary sizable great resources with a careful approach for an effective solution. Administrative and political authorities, Pope Francis underlines, must address this issue so they can help improve conditions for those who are suffering in hospital beds.

Faith in God plays a very important role in these situations, because it motivates the person, who may feel troubled and desperate, as if nothing makes sense when afflicted with a serious disease, illness, or sickness that tests the person's strength. Faith in God also instills the individual with optimism.

It is not a magic wand that makes pain and suffering disappear, but it certainly gives "a key by which we can discover the deepest meaning of what we are experiencing; a key that helps us to see how illness can be the way to draw nearer to Jesus who walks at our side, weighed down by the Cross. And this key is given to us by Mary, our Mother, who has known this way at first hand" (Message, September 15, 2015).

2013

Be Missionaries in Bringing the Peace of Christ to the Sick

To all people you bring the peace of Christ, and if they do not welcome it, you go ahead just the same. To the sick you bring healing, because God wants to heal man of every evil. How many missionaries do this, they sow life, health, comfort to the outskirts of the world. . . . Everyone must be a missionary, everyone can hear that call of Jesus and go forth and proclaim the Kingdom!

Angelus, July 7, 2013

Illness: Darker Moments of Life, But We Are Not Alone

Trust Christ, listen to him, follow in his footsteps. He never abandons us, not even in the darkest moments of our lives. He is our hope. . . . The Church is not distant from your troubles, but accompanies you with affection. The Lord is near you and he takes you by the hand. Look to him in your most difficult moments and he will give you consolation and hope. And trust in the maternal love of his Mother Mary.

Speech, Visit to St. Francis Hospital,
Rio de Janeiro, July 24, 2013

Avoiding the "Culture of Waste"

In a frail human being, each one of us is invited to recognize the face of the Lord, who in his human flesh experienced the indifference and solitude to which we so often condemn the poorest of the poor, whether in developing countries or in wealthy societies. Every child who, rather than being born, is condemned unjustly to being aborted, bears the face of Jesus Christ, bears the face of the Lord, who even before he was born, and then just after birth, experienced the world's rejection. . . . And every elderly person, even if he is ill or at the end of his days, bears the face of Christ. They cannot be discarded, as the "culture of waste" suggests!

Speech, September 20, 2013

The Sick Transmit Serenity to Those Who Visit Them

A mustard seed is tiny, yet Jesus says that faith this size, small but true and sincere, suffices to achieve what is humanly impossible, unthinkable. And it is true! We all know people who are simple, humble, but whose faith is so strong it can move mountains! Let us think, for example, of some mothers and fathers who face very difficult situations; or of some sick, and even gravely ill, people who transmit serenity to those who come to visit them. These people, because of their faith, do not boast about what they do, rather, as Jesus asks in the Gospel, they say: "We are unworthy servants; we have only done what was our duty" (Lk 17:10). How many people among us have such strong, humble faith, and what good they do!

Angelus, October 6, 2013

Enhance the Participation of the Sick in Christian Communities

In order to promote the effective inclusion of sick people in the Christian community and to inspire in them a strong sense of belonging, pastoral care—which is inclusive—is necessary in parishes and associations. It is a matter of truly esteeming the presence and witness of individuals who are frail and suffering, not only as recipients of the work of evangelization, but also as active subjects in this apostolic endeavor.

Speech, November 9, 2013

The Sick Are an Integral Part of the Church

Dear brothers and sisters who are sick, do not look upon yourselves only as the objects of solidarity and charity, but feel you are fully included in the life and mission of the Church. You have your own place, a specific role in the parish and in every sector of the Church. Your presence, which may be silent but is actually far more eloquent than many words, your prayer, the daily offering of your suffering in union with those of Jesus Crucified for the salvation of the world, the patient and even joyful acceptance of your condition, are a spiritual resource and a patrimony for every Christian community. Do not be ashamed to be a precious treasure of the Church!

Speech, November 9, 2013

Sick Elderly People Carry with Them the Memory and Wisdom of Life

The elderly have always been and still are protagonists in the Church. Today more than ever the Church must set an example for the whole of society that, despite their inevitable and sometimes grave "ailments," the elderly are always important; indeed, they are indispensable. They carry the memory and wisdom of life to hand down to others, and they participate fully in the Church's mission. Let us remember that, in God's eyes, human life always retains its value far beyond any discriminating vision.

Speech, November 23, 2013

The Dignity, Identity, and Needs of the Patient (Respect—in the Care of the Sick Person)

The provision of adequate assistance and services which respect the dignity, identity and needs of patients is important, but the support of those who assist them, whether family members or healthcare professionals, is also important. This is only possible within the context of trust and within an atmosphere of a mutually respectful relationship. Lived in this way, care becomes quite an enriching experience, both professionally and humanly; otherwise, it becomes all too similar to cold, basic "physical protection."

Speech, November 23, 2013

Silence in the Care Sector Becomes Torture

It therefore becomes necessary to be committed to a form of assistance that, alongside the traditional biomedical model, offers spaces of dignity and freedom, far, far away from closure and silence, that torture of silence! Silence is so often transformed into torture. People who live in assisted care are often surrounded by this sense of enclosure and silence. Within this perspective, I would like to stress the importance of the religious and spiritual aspect. Indeed, this is a dimension that remains vital even when cognitive faculties have been reduced or lost. It is a matter of implementing a special pastoral approach in order to accompany the religious life of elderly patients with serious degenerative diseases in various forms, to ensure that their minds and hearts do not interrupt their dialogue and relationship with God.

Speech, November 23, 2013

Suffering and Prayers

You do so much good for the Church through your suffering, inexplicable suffering. And God knows about these things and your prayers as well.

Speech, November 30, 2013

We Also Meet Jesus by Visiting the Sick Person

Our whole life is an encounter with Jesus: in prayer, when we go to Mass, and when we do good works, when we visit the sick, when we help the poor, when we think of others, when we are not selfish, when we are loving . . . in these things we always meet Jesus. And the journey of life is precisely this: journeying in order to meet Jesus.

Homily, December 1, 2013

The Presence of Christ in the Sick

The Church recognizes in you, the sick, a special presence of the suffering Christ. It is true. At the side of—and indeed within—our suffering, is the suffering of Christ; he bears its burden with us and he reveals its meaning. When the Son of God mounted the cross, he destroyed the solitude of suffering and illuminated its darkness. We thus find ourselves before the mystery of God's love for us, which gives us hope and courage: hope, because in the plan of God's love even the night of pain yields to the light of Easter, and courage, which enables us to confront every hardship in his company, in union with him.

Message for 2014 World Day of the Sick, December 6, 2013

Illness and Suffering

The incarnate Son of God did not remove illness and suffering from human experience but by taking them upon himself he transformed them and gave them new meaning. New meaning because they no longer have the last word which, instead, is new and abundant life; transformed them, because in union with Christ they need no longer be negative but positive.

Message for 2014 World Day of the Sick, December 6, 2013

Attending to Bring Hope

When we draw near with tender love to those in need of care, we bring hope and God's smile to the contradictions of the world. When generous devotion to others becomes the hallmark of our actions, we give way to the Heart of Christ and bask in its warmth, and thus contribute to the coming of God's Kingdom.

Message for 2014 World Day of the Sick, December 6, 2013

Mary, Mother of All the Sick

To grow in tender love, and a respectful and sensitive charity, we have a sure Christian model to contemplate: Mary, the Mother of Jesus and our Mother, who is always attentive to the voice of God and the needs and troubles of her children. Mary, impelled by God's mercy which took flesh within her, selflessly hastened from Galilee to Judea to find and help her kinswoman Elizabeth. She interceded with her Son at the wedding feast of Cana when she saw that there was a shortage of wine. She bore in her heart, throughout the pilgrimage of her life, the words of the elderly Simeon who foretold that a sword would pierce her soul, and with persevering strength she stood at the foot of the cross of Jesus. She knows the way, and for this reason she is the Mother of all of the sick and suffering. To her we can turn with confidence and filial devotion, certain that she will help us, support us and not abandon us. She is the Mother of the crucified and risen Christ: she stands beside our crosses and she accompanies us on the journey towards the resurrection and the fullness of life.

Message for 2014 World Day of the Sick, December 6, 2013

The Cross, Love, and the Mercy of God for Those Who Suffer

The cross is "the certainty of the faithful love which God has for us. A love so great that it enters into our sin and forgives it, enters into our suffering and gives us the strength to bear it. It is a love which enters into death to conquer it and to save us . . . the cross of Christ invites us also to allow ourselves to be smitten by his love, teaching us always to look upon others with mercy and tenderness, especially those who suffer, who are in need of help" (Way of the Cross with Young People, Rio de Janeiro, July 26, 2013).

Message for 2014 World Day of the Sick, December 6, 2013

2014

God's Preference for the Sick

Jesus in fact taught his disciples to have the same preferential love that he did for the sick and suffering, and he transmitted to them the ability and duty to continue providing, in his name and after his own heart, relief and peace through the special grace of this Sacrament [the Anointing of the Sick]. This, however, should not make us fall into an obsessive search for miracles or the presumption that one can always and in any situation be healed. Rather, it is the reassurance of Jesus' closeness to the sick and the aged, too, because any elderly person, anyone over the age of 65, can receive this Sacrament, through which Jesus himself draws close to us.

General Audience, February 26, 2014

The Priest Helps the Sick, Embracing the Person as God Would

When someone is sick, we at times think: "let's call for the priest to come"; "no, then he will bring bad luck, let's not call him," or "he will scare the sick person." Why do we think this? Because the idea is floating about that the undertakers arrive after the priest. And this is not true. The priest comes to help the sick or elderly person; that is why the priest's visit to the sick is so important; we ought to call the priest to the sick person's side and say: "come, give him the anointing, bless him." It is Jesus himself who comes to relieve the sick person, to give him strength, to give him hope, to help him; and also to forgive his sins. And this is very beautiful! And one must not think that this is taboo, because in times of pain and illness it is always good to know that we are not alone: the priest and those who are present during the Anointing of the Sick, in fact, represent the entire Christian community that as one body huddles around the one who suffers and his family, nurturing their faith and hope, and supporting them through their prayers and fraternal warmth. But the greatest comfort comes from the fact that it is the Lord Jesus himself who makes himself present in the Sacrament, who takes us by the hand, who caresses us as he did with the sick, and who reminds us that we already belong to him and that nothing—not even evil and death—can ever separate us from him. Are we in the habit of calling for the priest so that he might come to our sick—I am not speaking about those who are sick with the flu, for three or four days, but rather about a serious illness—and our elderly, and give them this

Sacrament, this comfort, this strength of Jesus to continue on? Let us do so!

General Audience, February 26, 2014

The Passion of Jesus Is the Greatest School to Dedicate Oneself to the Service of the Sick

It is true, in fact, that also in suffering no one is ever alone because God—in his merciful love for man and for the world—embraces even the most inhumane situations, in which the image of the Creator, present in everyone, is blurred or disfigured. Thus it was for Jesus in his Passion. In Him every human pain, every anxiety, every suffering was taken on out of love, out of pure desire to be close to us, to be with us. And here, in Jesus' Passion, is the greatest lesson for anyone who wants to dedicate him-herself to serving our sick and suffering brothers.

The experience of fraternal sharing with those who suffer opens us to the true beauty of human life which includes its frailty. In protecting and promoting life, at any stage or condition, we can recognize the dignity and value of every single human being, from conception until death.

Speech, March 24, 2014

Unity of Body and Spirit for an Integral View of Disease

But in order to talk about total health, it is necessary not to lose sight of the fact that the human person, created in the image and likeness of God, is a unity of body and spirit. The Greeks were more precise: body, soul and spirit. The human person is unity. These two elements may be distinguished but not separated, because the person is one. Thus also illness, the experience of pain and suffering, involves not only the physical dimension, but man in his totality. That is why there is need for integral treatment, which considers the person as a whole and joins medical care—"technical" care—to human, psychological and social support, for the physician has to care for all aspects: the human body in its psychological, social and spiritual dimensions, as well as the spiritual accompaniment and support for the sick person's family. It is, therefore, imperative that healthcare workers be those who are "led by an integrally human view of illness and who as a result are able to effect a fully human approach to the sick person who is suffering" (John Paul II, Motu Proprio *Dolentium hominum, Feb. 11, 1985).*

Speech, April 12, 2014

Share Moments with the Patient to Open Us Up to the Beauty of Life

Fraternal sharing with the sick opens us up to the true beauty of human life, which also includes its fragility, thus enabling us to recognize the dignity and value of every human being, in whatever situation they may find themselves, from conception to death.

Speech, April 12, 2014

There Are Those Who Cry Because They Have No Health: Jesus Has Known All Suffering

"Blessed are those who mourn, for they shall be comforted" (Mt 5:4). Jesus uses these prophetic words to refer to a condition of earthly life that affects everyone. There are people who cry because they do not have their health, people who cry because they are alone or misunderstood . . . there are so many things that cause suffering. Jesus himself experienced affliction and humiliation in this world. He took human sufferings, took them on in his own flesh, and experienced them fully one by one. He knew every kind of affliction, both moral and physical. He experienced hunger and fatigue and the bitterness of misunderstanding. He was betrayed and abandoned, scourged and crucified.

Speech, May 17, 2014

Experiencing Suffering with Trust and Hope

When he says, "blessed are those who mourn," Jesus does not intend to declare an unfavorable and difficult condition of life felicitous. Suffering is not a value in itself but a reality that Jesus teaches us to live with the right attitude. There are, in fact, right ways and wrong ways to experience pain and suffering. The wrong attitude is experiencing pain passively, letting ourselves be swept up in inertia and giving up. Reacting with rebellion and denial is not the correct attitude either. Jesus teaches us to experience pain by accepting the reality of life with trust and hope and *by putting the love of God and our neighbors too into suffering*: it is love that transforms all things.

Speech, May 17, 2014

Move Closer to the Suffering to Enrich the Church

With this charism, you are a gift for the Church. Your sufferings, like Jesus' wounds, are a scandal for faith, yet they are also the test of faith. They are the sign that God is Love, that He is faithful, that He is merciful, that He is a consoler. United to the Risen Christ, you are "active participants in the work of evangelization and salvation" (Apostolic Exhortation *Christifideles laici*, 54). I encourage you to be close to those in your parishes who are suffering, as witnesses of the Resurrection. In this way, you enrich the Church and collaborate in the mission of pastors by praying and offering up your sufferings for them as well.

Speech, May 17, 2014

To Test the Love of God Even in Sickness

Jesus did not come to conquer men like the kings and the powerful of this world, but He came to offer love with gentleness and humility. . . . We can experience and savour the tenderness of this love at every stage of life: in times of joy and of sadness, in times of good health and of frailty and those of sickness.

Homily, June 27, 2014

Only in God Is the Strength of the Sick Person

I really think of you sick people, tended with love and professionalism . . . in prayer, cultivate a taste for the matters of God, be witnesses that your strength lies in God alone. You sick persons, who experience the fragility of the body, can witness with strength to people who are nearby, how life's precious resource is the Gospel and the Father's merciful love, not money or power. Indeed, even when a person is, according to worldly logic, important, he cannot add a single day to his own life.

Video Message, July 13, 2014

Draw Closer to God by Serving the Sick

Keep close to one another, draw ever closer to God, and with your bishops and priests spend these years in building a holier, more missionary and humble Church . . . a

Church which loves and worships God by seeking to serve
the poor, the lonely, the infirm and the marginalized.

Homily, August 17, 2014

Charity Toward the Sick Person Requires Time to Take Care of the Person and Time to Visit Him or Her

*Wisdom of the heart means showing solidarity with our brothers and
sisters while not judging them.* Charity takes time. Time to care
for the sick and time to visit them. Time to be at their side
like Job's friends: "And they sat with him on the ground
seven days and seven nights, and no one spoke a word to
him, for they saw that his suffering was very great" (Job
2:13). Yet Job's friends harbored a judgment against him:
they thought that Job's misfortune was a punishment
from God for his sins. True charity is a sharing which
does not judge, which does not demand the conversion of
others; it is free of that false humility which, deep down,
seeks praise and is self-satisfied about whatever good
it does.

Message, December 3, 2014

The Experience of Pain and Sickness Strengthen the Wisdom of the Heart

Even when illness, loneliness and inability make it hard for us to reach out to others, the experience of suffering can become a privileged means of transmitting grace and a source for gaining and growing in *sapientia cordis*. We come to understand how Job, at the end of his experience, could say to God: "I had heard of you by the hearing of the ear, but now my eye sees you" (42:5).

Message, December 3, 2014

The Mystery of Suffering and Pain Is Faced with Faith

People immersed in the mystery of suffering and pain, when they accept these in faith, can themselves become living witnesses of a faith capable of embracing suffering, even without being able to understand its full meaning.

Message, December 3, 2014

The Closeness of the Lord for Continuous Care of the Sick

Today too, how many Christians show, not by their words but by lives rooted in a genuine faith, that they are "eyes to the blind" and "feet to the lame"! They are close to the sick in need of constant care and help in washing, dressing and eating. This service, especially when it is protracted, can become tiring and burdensome. It is relatively easy to help someone for a few days but it is difficult to look after a person for months or even years, in some cases when he or she is no longer capable of expressing gratitude. And yet, what a great path of sanctification this is! In those difficult moments we can rely in a special way on the closeness of the Lord, and we become a special means of support for the Church's mission.

Message, December 3, 2014

The Special Value of the Moments Spent Next to the Sick

Wisdom of the heart means going forth from ourselves toward our brothers and sisters. Occasionally our world forgets the special value of time spent at the bedside of the sick, since we are in such a rush; caught up as we are in a frenzy of doing, of producing, we forget about giving ourselves freely, taking care of others, being responsible for others. Behind this attitude there is often a lukewarm faith which has forgotten the Lord's words: "You did it unto me' (Mt 25:40).

Message, December 3, 2014

Holy Time Is Spent Near the Sick

Wisdom of the heart means being with our brothers and sisters. Time spent with the sick is holy time. It is a way of praising God who conforms us to the image of his Son, who "came not to be served but to serve, and to give his life as a ransom for many" (Mt 20:28). Jesus himself said: "I am among you as one who serves" (Lk 22:27).

Message, December 3, 2014

2015

Learn from Families Who Have Children with Disabilities

When it comes to the challenges of communication, *families who have children with one or more disabilities* have much to teach us. A motor, sensory or mental *limitation* can be a reason for closing in on ourselves, but it can also become, thanks to the love of parents, siblings, and friends, an *incentive to openness, sharing and ready communication with all*. It can also help schools, parishes and associations to become more welcoming and inclusive of everyone.

Message, January 23, 2015

The Path of the Church Is to Leave One's Own Encloure and Go to Meet the Sick

The way of the Church is not to condemn anyone for eternity; to pour out the balm of God's mercy on all those who ask for it with a sincere heart. The way of the Church is precisely to leave her four walls behind and to go out in search of those who are distant, those essentially on the "outskirts" of life. It is to adopt fully God's own approach, to follow the Master who said: "Those who are well have no need of the physician, but those who are sick; I have come to call, not the righteous but sinners" (Lk 5:31-32).

Homily, February 15, 2015

Charity Heals

Charity cannot be neutral, antiseptic, indifferent, lukewarm or impartial! Charity is infectious, it excites, it risks and it engages! For true charity is always unmerited, unconditional and gratuitous! (cf. 1 Cor 13). Charity is creative in finding the right words to speak to all those considered incurable and hence untouchable.

Homily, February 15, 2015

Support for Palliative Care

The objective of palliative care is to alleviate suffering in the final stages of illness and at the same time to ensure the patient appropriate human accompaniment (cf. Encyclical *Evangelium Vitae*, no. 65). It is important support especially for the elderly, who, because of their age, receive increasingly less attention from curative medicine and are often abandoned. Abandonment is the most serious "illness" of the elderly, and also the greatest injustice they can be submitted to: those who have helped us grow must not be abandoned when they are in need of our help, our love and our tenderness.

Speech, March 5, 2015

We Must Not Be Ashamed of Going to See a Sick Person

It isn't easy to reach out to a sick person. Life's most beautiful things and most miserable things are modest, are hidden. Out of modesty, one tries to hide the greatest love; and out of modesty, we also seek to hide the things that show our human misery. This is why, when visiting a sick person, it is necessary to go to him or her, because the modesty of life hides them. Visit the sick. And when there are lifelong illnesses, when we have diseases that mark an entire life, we prefer to hide them, because to visit a sick person means visiting our own illness, that which we have inside. It is having the courage to say to oneself: I too have some disease in my heart, in my soul, in my spirit, I too am spiritually ill.

Speech, March 21, 2015

One Can Face and Understand an Illness Only in the Spirit of Faith

God created us to change the world, to be efficient, to rule over Creation: it is our task. But when we are confronted with disease, we see that this illness prevents this: that man, that woman who was born that way, or whose body has become that way, it is like saying "no"— seemingly—to the mission of transforming the world. This is the mystery of sickness. One can approach illness only in the spirit of faith. We can draw near to a sick man, woman, boy or girl, only if we look to Him who took all of our sickness upon Himself, if we become accustomed to looking at Christ Crucified. The only explanation for this "failure," this human failure, a lifetime of sickness, is there. The only explanation is in Christ Crucified.

Speech, March 21, 2015

The Sick Are the Brothers and Sisters Who Are Closest to Christ

I say to you, sick people, that if you cannot understand the Lord, I ask the Lord to enable you to understand in your heart that you are the flesh of Christ, that you are Christ Crucified among us, that you are the brothers and sisters closest to Christ. It is one thing to look at a Crucifix and it's another thing to look at a man, woman, child who is sick, in other words crucified there in their illness: they are the living flesh of Christ.

Speech, March 21, 2015

The Sick Reflect the Suffering Christ

The world of illness is a world of pain. Sick people suffer, they reflect the suffering Christ: there is no need to fear drawing near to Christ who is suffering.

Speech, March 21, 2015

The Family Is the Nearest Hospital

Within the realm of family bonds, the illness of our loved ones is endured with an "excess" of suffering and anguish. It is love that makes us feel this "excess." So often for a father or a mother, it is more difficult to bear a son or daughter's the pain than one's own. The family, we can say, has always been the nearest "hospital." Still today, in so many parts of the world, a hospital is for the privileged few, and is often far away. It is the mother, the father, brothers, sisters and grandparents who guarantee care and help one to heal.

General Audience, June 10, 2015

Jesus Always Heals Humanity from Illness

In the Gospels, many pages tell of Jesus' encounters with the sick and of his commitment to healing them. He presents himself publicly as one who fights against illness and who has come to heal mankind of every evil: evils of the spirit and evils of the body. The Gospel scene just referenced from the Gospel according to Mark is truly moving. It says: "That evening, at sundown, they brought to him all who were sick or possessed with demons" (1:32). When I think of today's great cities, I wonder where are the doors to which the sick are brought hoping to be healed! Jesus never held back from their care. He never passed by, never turned his face away. When a father or mother, or even just friends brought a sick person for him to touch and heal, he never let time be an issue; healing came before the law, even one as sacred as resting on the Sabbath (cf. Mk 3:1-6). The doctors of the law reproached Jesus because he healed on the Sabbath, he did good on the Sabbath. But the love of Jesus was in giving health, doing good: this always takes priority!

General Audience, June 10, 2015

The Church's Mission Is to Stay Close to the Sick Person

Jesus sends his disciples to perform the same work and gives them the power to heal, in other words, to draw close to the sick and to heal their deepest wounds (cf. Mt 10:1). We must keep in mind what he says to the disciples in the episode of the man blind from birth (Jn 9:1-5). The disciples—with the blind man there in front of them!—argue about who sinned, this man or his parents, that he was born blind, causing his blindness. The Lord says clearly: neither him nor his parents; he is so in order that the works of God be made manifest in him. And He heals him. This is the glory of God! This is the Church's task! To help the sick, not to get lost in gossip, always help, comfort, relieve, be close to the sick; this is the task.

General Audience, June 10, 2015

Prayer for the Sick Must Be Continuous

The Church invites constant prayer for her own loved ones stricken with suffering. There must never be a lack of prayer for the sick. But rather, we must pray more, both personally and as a community. Let us consider the Gospel episode of the Canaanite woman (cf. Mt 15:21-28). She is a pagan woman. She is not of the People of Israel, but a pagan who implores Jesus to heal her daughter. To test her faith, Jesus at first responds harshly: "I cannot, I must think first of the sheep of Israel." The woman does not give up—when a mother asks for help for her infant, she never gives up; we all know that mothers fight for their children—and she replies: "even dogs are given something when their masters have eaten," as if to say: "At least treat me like a dog!" Thus Jesus says to her: "woman, great is your faith! Be it done for you as you desire" (v. 28).

General Audience, June 10, 2015

Educate in the Family to Understand Illness

In the face of illness, even in families, difficulties arise due to human weakness. But in general, times of illness enable family bonds to grow stronger. I think about how important it is to teach children, starting from childhood, about solidarity in times of illness. An education which protects against sensitivity for human illness withers the heart. It allows young people to be "anaesthetized" against the suffering of others, incapable of facing suffering and of living the experience of limitation. How often do we see a man or woman arrive at work with a weary face, with a tired countenance and, when we ask them "What happened?," they answer: "I only slept two hours because we are taking turns at home to be close to our boy, our girl, our sick one, our grandfather, our grandmother." And the day of work goes on. These are heroic deeds, the heroism of families! That hidden heroism carried out with tenderness and courage when someone at home is sick.

General Audience, June 10, 2015

The Family, in the Test of Sickness, Should Not Be Left Alone

The weakness and suffering of our dearest and most cherished loved ones can be, for our children and grandchildren, a school of life—it's important to teach the children, the grandchildren to understand this closeness in illness at home—and they become so when times of illness are accompanied by prayer and the affectionate and thoughtful closeness of relatives. The Christian community really knows that the family, in the trial of illness, should not be left on its own. We must say 'thank you' to the Lord for those beautiful experiences of ecclesial fraternity that help families get through the difficult moments of pain and suffering. This Christian closeness, from family to family, is a real treasure for the parish; a treasure of wisdom, which helps families in the difficult moments to understand the Kingdom of God better than many discourses! They are God's caresses.

General Audience, June 10, 2015

Disabled People, the Elderly, Must Not Be Victims of the "Culture of Waste"

The exclusion of the poor and the difficulty for the indigent to receive assistance and necessary treatment, is a situation which is unfortunately still present today. Great advancements have been made in medicine and in social assistance, but a throw-away culture has also spread, as a consequence of an anthropological crisis which no longer places mankind at the center, but consumerism and economic interests (cf. Apostolic Exhortation *Evangelii Gaudium*, nos. 52-53).

Among the victims of this throw-away culture, I would like to remember here in particular the elderly, so many of whom have been welcomed in this home; the elderly are the memory and the wisdom of peoples. Their longevity is not always seen as a gift of God, but at times as a difficult burden to bear, especially when their health is seriously compromised. This mindset does not do society any good, and it is our task to develop an "antidote" to this way of considering the elderly, or people with disabilities, almost as if they were lives no longer worth living. This is a sin, it is a grave social sin. Instead with such tenderness Cottolengo* loved these people! Here we can learn another way of looking at life and at the human person!

Speech, June 21, 2015

*St. Joseph Benedict Cottolengo

Faith Is Key to Approaching God in Sickness

Illness, above all grave illness, always places human existence in crisis and brings with it questions that dig deep.

Our first response may at times be one of rebellion: Why has this happened to me? We can feel desperate, thinking that all is lost, that things no longer have meaning . . .

In these situations, faith in God is on the one hand tested, yet at the same time can reveal all of its positive resources. Not because faith makes illness, pain, or the questions which they raise, disappear, but because it offers a key by which we can discover the deepest meaning of what we are experiencing; a key that helps us to see how illness can be the way to draw nearer to Jesus who walks at our side, weighed down by the Cross. And this key is given to us by Mary, our Mother, who has known this way at first hand.

Message, September 15, 2015

Mary Opens Us to Mercy Toward the Sick Person

We have a Mother with benevolent and watchful eyes, like her Son; a heart that is maternal and full of mercy, like him; hands that want to help, like the hands of Jesus who broke bread for those who were hungry, touched the sick and healed them. All this fills us with trust and opens our hearts to the grace and mercy of Christ.

Message, September 15, 2015

The Mercy of the Lord
Toward the Sick Person

At Cana the distinctive features of Jesus and his mission
are clearly seen: he comes to the help of those in difficulty
and need. Indeed, in the course of his messianic ministry he would heal many people of illnesses, infirmities
and evil spirits, give sight to the blind, make the lame
walk, restore health and dignity to lepers, raise the dead,
and proclaim the good news to the poor (cf. Lk 7:21-22).
Mary's request at the wedding feast, suggested by the
Holy Spirit to her maternal heart, clearly shows not only
Jesus' messianic power but also his mercy.

Message, September 15, 2015

Understanding the Needs of the
Sick with Love and Tenderness

In Mary's concern we see reflected the tenderness of God.
This same tenderness is present in the lives of all those
persons who attend the sick and understand their needs,

even the most imperceptible ones, because they look upon them with eyes full of love.

Message, September 15, 2015

Helping Those Suffering in Sickness

We too can be hands, arms and hearts which help God to perform his miracles, so often hidden. We too, whether healthy or sick, can offer up our toil and sufferings like the water which filled the jars at the wedding feast of Cana and was turned into the finest wine. By quietly helping those who suffer, as in illness itself, we take our daily cross upon our shoulders and follow the Master (cf. Lk 9:23). Even though the experience of suffering will always remain a mystery, Jesus helps us to reveal its meaning.

Message, September 15, 2015

The Culture of Encounter with the Sick Person

Every hospital and nursing home can be a visible sign and setting in which to promote the culture of encounter and peace, where the experience of illness and suffering, along with professional and fraternal assistance, helps to overcome every limitation and division.

Message, September 15, 2015

Tenderness and Faith for the Sick and Those Who Suffer

Our revolution comes about through tenderness, through the joy which always becomes closeness and compassion—which is not pity, but suffering with, so as to free—and leads us to get involved in, and to serve, the life of others. Our faith makes us leave our homes and go forth to encounter others, to share their joys, their hopes and their frustrations. Our faith, "calls us out of our house," to visit the sick, the prisoner and to those who mourn. It makes us able to laugh with those who laugh, and rejoice with our neighbors who rejoice.

Homily, (Cuba), September 22, 2015

Interpreters of the Cry for Human Dignity

The anxiety that the Church harbors is for the fate of the human family and of all of creation. It is about educating everyone to "care for" and to "administer" Creation as a whole, as a gift entrusted to the responsibility of every generation, so that it is handed down as intact and humanly liveable as possible to the coming generations. This conversion of heart to the "Gospel of Creation" implies that we make our own and render ourselves interpreters of the cry for human dignity, which is raised above all by the poorest and most excluded, as sick and suffering people often are.

Speech, November 19, 2015

2016

The Effective Help of Mercy for Every Infirmity

In God's mercy, all of our infirmities find healing. His mercy, in fact, does not keep a distance: it seeks to encounter all forms of poverty and to free this world of so many types of slavery. Mercy desires to reach the wounds of all, to heal them. Being *apostles of mercy* means touching and soothing the wounds that today afflict the bodies and souls of many of our brothers and sisters. Curing these wounds, we profess Jesus, we make him present and alive; we allow others, who touch his mercy with their own hands, to recognize him as "Lord and God" (Jn 20:28), as did the Apostle Thomas. This is the mission that he entrusts to us. So many people ask to be *listened to and to be understood*. The Gospel of mercy, to be proclaimed and written in our daily lives, seeks people with patient and open hearts, "good Samaritans" who understand compassion and silence before the mystery of each brother and sister. The Gospel of mercy requires generous and joyful servants, people who love freely without expecting anything in return.

Homily, April 3, 2016

Hospitality and Attention in the Church to the Various Forms of Disability

In the Church, thanks be to God, one notes widespread attention to disability in its physical, mental and sensory forms, and an attitude of general acceptance. However, our communities still find it hard to exercise a true inclusion, a full participation that may at last become ordinary, normal. It calls for not only specific techniques and programs, but it requires first of all that each face be recognized and accepted, with the tenacious and patient certainty that every person is unique and unrepeatable, and that every excluded face is an impoverishment of the community.

Speech, June 11, 2016

Attention in Christian Communities to People with Disabilities

May our Christian communities be "houses" in which every form of suffering finds compassion, in which every family with its burden of pain and toil may feel under-stood and respected in its dignity. As I observed in the

Apostolic Exhortation *Amoris Laetitia*, the "dedication and concern shown to migrants and to persons with special needs alike is a sign of the Spirit. Both situations are paradigmatic: they serve as a test of our commitment to show mercy in welcoming others and to help the vulnerable to be fully a part of our communities" (no. 47).

Speech, June 11, 2016

The Sacraments and Persons with Disabilities

The inclusion of the disabled through their admission to the sacraments is naturally decisive. If we recognize the particularity and the beauty of their experience of Christ and of the Church, we must as a result clearly affirm that they are called to the fullness of sacramental life, even in the presence of serious psychic dysfunction. It is sad to discover that in some cases doubts, resistance and even rejection persist. Often one justifies the rejection by saying: "he does not understand anyway," or: "she does not need it." In reality, with this attitude, one shows that he or she does not truly understand the significance of the Sacraments themselves, and in fact denies disabled people the practice of their divine adoption and full participation in the ecclesial community.

Speech, June 11, 2016

One Can Find Strength Amidst Illness

The way we experience illness and disability is an index of the love we are ready to offer. The way we face suffering and limitation is the measure of our freedom to give meaning to life's experiences, even when they strike us as meaningless and unmerited. Let us not be disturbed, then, by these tribulations (cf. 1 *Thes 3:3*). *We know that in weakness we can become strong (cf. 2 Cor 12:10) and receive the grace to fill up what is lacking in the sufferings of Christ for his body, the Church (cf. Col 1:24). For that body, in the image of the risen Lord's own, keeps its wounds, the mark of a hard struggle, but they are wounds transfigured for ever by love.*

Homily, June 12, 2016

The Meaning of Life Includes the Acceptance of Suffering

Human nature, wounded by sin, is marked by *limitations*. We are familiar with the objections raised, especially nowadays, to a life characterized by serious physical limitations. It is thought that sick or disabled persons cannot be happy, since they cannot live the lifestyle held up by the culture of pleasure and entertainment. In an age when care for one's body has become an obsession and a big business, anything imperfect has to be hidden away, since it threatens the happiness and serenity of the privileged few and endangers the dominant model. Such persons should best be kept apart, in some "enclosure"—even a gilded one—or in "islands" of pietism or social welfare, so that they do not hold back the pace of a false well-being. In some cases, we are even told that it is better to eliminate them as soon as possible, because they become an unacceptable economic burden in time of crisis. Yet what an illusion it is when people today shut their eyes in the face of sickness and disability! They fail to understand the real meaning of life, which also has to do with accepting suffering and limitations. The world does not become better because only apparently "perfect" people live there—I say "perfect" rather than "false"—but when human solidarity, mutual acceptance and respect increase. How true are the words of the Apostle: "God chose what is weak in the world to shame the strong" (1 Cor *1:27*)!

Homily, June 12, 2016

Smile Therapy

The happiness that everyone desires, for that matter, can be expressed in any number of ways and attained only if we are capable of loving. This is the way. It is always a matter of love; there is no other path. The true challenge is that of who loves the most. How many disabled and suffering persons open their hearts to life again as soon as they realize they are loved! How much love can well up in a heart simply with a smile! The therapy of smiling. Then our frailness itself can become a source of consolation and support in our solitude. Jesus, in his passion, loved us to the end (cf. Jn 13:1); on the cross he revealed the love that bestows itself without limits. Can we reproach God for our infirmities and sufferings when we realize how much suffering shows on the face of his crucified Son? His physical pain was accompanied by mockery, condescension and scorn, yet he responds with a mercy that accepts and forgives everything: "by his wounds we are healed" (Is 53:5; 1 Pet 2:24). Jesus is the physician who heals with the medicine of love, for he takes upon himself our suffering and redeems it. We know that God can understand our infirmities, because he himself has personally experienced them (cf. Heb 4:15).

Homily, June 6, 2016

The Study of the Sciences to Serve the Sick

Nature, in all its complexity, and the human mind, are created by God; their richness must be studied by skilled men and women, in the knowledge that the advancement of the philosophical and empirical sciences, as well as professional care in favor of the weakest and most infirm, is a service that is part of God's plan. Openness to the grace of God, an openness which comes through faith, does not weaken human reason, but rather leads it to move forwards, to knowledge of a truth which is wider and of greater benefit to humanity.

Speech, August 31, 2016

Just a Smile to Cheer the Sick

The Church views closeness to those who suffer as her task and her responsibility, so as to bring them consolation, comfort and friendship. . . . You dedicate your life above all to the service of brothers and sisters who are hospitalized, so that thanks to your presence and professionalism they feel better supported during their illness. And to do this, there is no need for long speeches: a caress, a kiss, staying close to someone in silence, a smile. Never give up in this service, which is so valuable, despite all the difficulties you may encounter. At times, in our days, a secular culture aims to remove all religious reference from hospitals, starting from the very presence of women religious. When this happens, though, it is accompanied not infrequently by a painful lack of humanity, truly strident in places of suffering. Never tire of being friends, sisters and mothers to the sick; may prayer always be the vital lymph that supports your evangelizing mission.

Speech, September 24, 2016

Jesus Is Present in That Person Who Suffers

When you are close to every ailing person, keep in your heart the peace and the joy that are the fruit of the Holy Spirit. On that hospital bed there always lies Jesus, present in the person who suffers, and it is He Who asks for help from each one of you. It is Jesus. At times one might think, "Some patients are bothersome." But we too are bothersome to the Lord, and He supports us and accompanies us! May closeness to Jesus and to the weakness be your strength.

Speech, September 24, 2016

Eloquent and Effective Expressions of Mercy

Jesus' life, especially during the three years of his public ministry, was a continual encounter with people. Among them, the sick had a special place. How many pages of the Gospel tell of these encounters! The paralytic, the blind man, the leper, the possessed man, the epileptic, and the countless people suffering from illnesses of every kind. . . . Jesus made himself close to each of them, and cured them with his presence and his healing power. Therefore, among the works of mercy, we cannot fail to visit and assist those who are sick. . . .

With this work of mercy, the Lord invites us to make an act of great humanity: *sharing.* Let us remember this word: sharing. Those who are sick often feel alone. We cannot hide the fact that, especially in our days, in sickness one experiences greater loneliness than at other times in life. A visit can make a person who is sick feel less alone, and a little companionship is great medicine! A smile, a caress, a handshake are simple gestures, but they are very important for those who feel abandoned. How many people dedicate themselves to visiting the sick in hospitals or in their homes! It is a priceless voluntary work. When it is done in the Lord's name, moreover, it also becomes an *eloquent and effective expression of mercy*. Let us not leave the sick alone! Let us not prevent them from finding consolation, or ourselves from being enriched by our closeness to those who suffer. Hospitals are true "cathedrals of suffering" where, however, the power of supportive and compassionate charity is also made evident.

General Audience, November 9, 2016

Every Human Person Is Worthy of Being Welcomed and Treated

If the human person is the eminent value, it follows that each person, above all a person who suffers, because of a "rare" or "neglected" disease as well, without any hesitation deserves every kind of commitment in order to be welcomed, treated and, if possible, healed.

Message, November 12, 2016

The "Wisdom of the Heart" to Deal with "Rare and Neglected" Diseases

The effective addressing of entire chapters of illness, as is the case with "rare" and "neglected" diseases, requires not only qualified and diversified skills and abilities in health-care but also ones that are beyond health care—one may think of health-care managers, of administrative and political health-care authorities, and of health-care economists. An integrated approach, and careful assessments of contexts directed towards the planning and implementation of operational strategies, as well as the obtaining and management of the necessary sizeable resources, are required. At the base of every initiative, however, lies, first and foremost, free and courageous good will directed towards the solving of this major problem of global health: an authentic "wisdom of the heart." Together with scientific and technical study, the determination and wisdom of those who set themselves to work not only in the existential fringes of the world but also in its fringes at the level of care, as is of often the case with "rare" and "neglected" diseases, are, therefore, crucial.

Message, November 12, 2016

Key Words for the Person Who Suffers: Inform, Care, and Steward

Amongst the many who give of themselves generously, the Church, as well, has always been active in this field and will continue with this exacting and demanding pathway of nearness to, and the accompanying of, the person who suffers. It is no accident, therefore, that this thirty-first international conference* wanted to adopt the following key words to communicate the sense—understood as meaning and direction—of the presence of the Church in this authentic work of mercy: *to inform*, in order to establish the state of present knowledge at a scientific and clinical/care level; *to care for the life of patients in a better way in a welcoming and supportive approach; to steward* the environment in which man lives.

Message, November 12, 2016

* International Conference on Rare Pathologies Organized by the Pontifical Council for Health Care Workers

Respect and Stewardship of Creation to Avoid the Damage of Many Rare Diseases

Many diseases have genetic causes; in the case of others, environmental factors have a major importance. But even when the causes are genetic, a polluted environment acts as a multiplier of damage. And the greatest burden falls on the poorest populations. It is for this reason that I want once again to emphasise the absolute importance of respect for, and the stewardship of, the creation, our common home.

Message, November 12, 2016

The Church Is a "Field Hospital"

It remains a priority of the Church to keep herself dynamically in a state of "moving outwards," to bear witness at a concrete level to divine mercy, making herself a "field hospital" for marginalised people who live in every existential, socio-economic, health-care, environmental and geographical fringe of the world.

Message, November 12, 2016

The Basic Principles of the Church's Social Doctrine on Sickness

Although it is true that care for a person with a "rare" or "neglected" disease is in large measure connected with the interpersonal relationship of the doctor and the patient, it is equally true that the approach, at a social level, to this health-care phenomenon requires a clear application of justice, in the sense of "giving to each his or her due," that is to say equal access to effective care for equal health needs, independently of factors connected with socio-economic, geographical or cultural contexts. The reason for this rests on three fundamental principles of the social doctrine of the Church. The first is the principle of *sociality*, according to which the good of the person reverberates through the entire community. Therefore, care for health is not only a responsibility entrusted to the stewardship of the person himself or herself. It is also a social good, in the sense that the more individual health grows, the more "collective health" will benefit from this, not least at the level, as well, of the resources that are freed up for other chapters of illness that require demanding research and treatment. The second principle is that of *subsidiarity* which, on the one hand, supports, promotes and develops socially the capacity of each person in attaining fulfilment and his or her legitimate and good aspirations, and, on the other, comes to the aid of a person where he or she is not able on his or her own to overcome possible obstacles, as is the case, for example, with an illness. And the third principle, with which a health-care strategy should be marked, and which must take the person as a value and the common good into account, is that of *solidarity*.

Message, November 12, 2016

Let Us Open Our Hearts to God to Pray and Give Help to the Sick

How many different ways there are to pray for our neighbor! They are all valid and accepted by God if done from the heart. . . . I think of praying for sick people, when we go to visit them and pray for them; of silent intercession, at times tearful, in the many difficult situations which require prayer. . . . Therefore, let us open our heart, to enable the Holy Spirit, scrutinizing our deepest aspirations, to purify them and lead them to fulfillment. However, for us and for others, let us always ask that God's will be done, as in the *Our Father*, because his will is surely the greatest good, the goodness of a Father who never abandons us: pray and let the Holy Spirit pray in us. This is beautiful in life: to pray, thanking and praising the Lord, asking for something, weeping when there are difficulties . . . But let the heart always be open to the Spirit, that he may pray in us, with us and for us.

General Audience, November 30, 2016

Love God and Also Our Brothers and Sisters Who Are in the Experience of the Illness

Even now, I am spiritually present at the grotto of Massabielle, before the statue of the Immaculate Virgin, in whom *the Almighty has done great things* for the redemption of mankind. I express my closeness to all of you, our suffering brothers and sisters, and to your families, as well as my appreciation for all those in different roles of service and in healthcare institutions throughout the world who work with professionalism, responsibility and dedication for your care, treatment and daily well-being. I encourage all of you, the sick, the suffering, physicians, nurses, family members and volunteers, to see in Mary, *Health of the Infirm*, the sure sign of God's love for every human being and a model of surrender to his will. May you always find in faith, nourished by the Word and by the Sacraments, the strength needed to love God, even in the experience of illness.

Message for World Day of the Sick 2017, December 8, 2016

Every Sick Person Has His or Her Dignity and Mission in Life

Every person is, and always remains, a human being, and is to be treated as such. The sick and those who are disabled, even severely, have their own inalienable dignity and mission in life. They never become simply objects. If at times they appear merely passive, in reality that is never the case.

Message for World Day of the Sick 2017, December 8, 2016

The Sick Person Carries His or Her Gift to Be Shared with Others

The fact that the Lovely Lady asked her to pray for sinners reminds us that the infirm and the suffering desire not only to be healed, but also to live a truly Christian life, even to the point of offering it as authentic missionary disciples of Christ. Mary gave Bernadette the vocation of serving the sick and called her to become a Sister of Charity, a mission that she carried out in so exemplary a way as to become a model for every healthcare worker. Let us ask Mary Immaculate for the grace always to relate to the sick as persons who certainly need assistance, at times even for the simplest of things, but who have a gift of their own to share with others.

Message for World Day of the Sick 2017, December 8, 2016

The Strength of Hope That Makes Us Get Up and Supports Us

The gaze of Mary, *Comfort of the Afflicted*, brightens the face of the Church in her daily commitment to the suffering and those in need. The precious fruits of this solicitude for the world of suffering and sickness are a reason for gratitude to the Lord Jesus, who out of obedience to the will of the Father became one of us, even enduring death on the cross for the redemption of humanity. The solidarity shown by Christ, the Son of God born of Mary, is the expression of God's merciful omnipotence, which is made manifest in our life—above all when that life is frail, pain-filled, humbled, marginalized and suffering—and fills it with the power of hope that can sustain us and enable us to get up again.

Message for World Day of the Sick 2017, December 8, 2016

Culture of Health and the Environment

On this World Day of the Sick, may we find new incentive to work for the growth of a culture of respect for life, health and the environment. May this Day also inspire renewed efforts to defend the integrity and dignity of persons, not least through a correct approach to bioethical issues, the protection of the vulnerable and the protection of the environment.

Message for World Day of the Sick 2017, December 8, 2016

Always Be the Joyful Presence of the Love of God for the Sick Person

On this Twenty-fifth World Day of the Sick, I once more offer my prayerful support and encouragement to physicians, nurses, volunteers and all those consecrated men and women committed to serving the sick and those in need. I also embrace the ecclesial and civil institutions working to this end, and the families who take loving care of their sick. I pray that all may be ever joyous signs of the presence of God's love and imitate the luminous testimony of so many friends of God, including St. John of God and St. Camillus de' Lellis, the patrons of hospitals and healthcare workers, and St. Mother Teresa of Calcutta, missionary of God's love.

Message for World Day of the Sick 2017, December 8, 2016

2017

Jesus Is with the Sick

Everyone has a problem, or a sickness, or a worry. Even children . . . There are things that cannot be explained, but which happen; life is like this. Jesus wanted to be close to us in our pain too; He said it Himself: "I was sick and you visited me." Jesus stays with the sick, with those who have problems. It is true. I know that when you suffer, when you have problems it is difficult to understand. However it is not a matter of understanding, but rather of feeling Jesus' caresses.

Homily, Meeting with the Sick, January 15, 2017

Life Is Sacred

Every life is sacred! Let us go forward with the culture of life to counter the logic of waste and the declining birth rate; let us be close and together let us pray for the babies who are threatened by the termination of pregnancy, as well as for the people who are at the end of life—every life is sacred!—so that no one may be left alone and that love may defend the meaning of life. Let us recall the words of Mother Teresa: "Life is beautiful, admire it; life is life, defend it!," be it a baby who is about to be born, or a person who is close to death: every life is sacred!

Angelus, February 5, 2017

Optimize Available Resources

If there is a sector in which the throwaway culture is manifest, with its painful consequences, it is that of healthcare. When a sick person is not placed in the center or their dignity is not considered, this gives rise to attitudes that can lead even to speculation on the misfortune of others. And this is very grave! It is necessary to be vigilant, especially when patients are elderly with gravely compromised health, if they are affected by illnesses that are serious or require burdensome cures, or are particularly difficult to treat, such as psychiatric patients. The application of a business approach to the healthcare sector, if indiscriminate, instead of optimizing resources may risk discarding human beings. Optimizing resources means using them in an ethical and fraternal way, and not penalizing the most fragile.

Speech, Februarly 10, 2017

The Protection of the Rights of the Weakest

There is the inviolable dignity of every human being from the moment of conception until the final breath (cf. Message for the 25th World Day of the Sick, December 8, 2016). May it not only be money [that guides] political and administrative decisions, called to safeguard the right to health ... nor the choices of those who manage healthcare structures. The increasing health poverty among the poorest sectors of the population, due precisely to the difficulty of access to care, must not leave anyone indifferent; may all efforts be redoubled to ensure the rights of the weakest are protected.

Speech, February 10, 2017

Pastoral Care for the Sick

Among the aims that St. John Paul II outlined for World Day of the Sick, aside from the promotion of the Culture of Life, there is also the involvement of the dioceses, Christian communities and religious families regarding the importance of health pastoral care, Pope Francis noted, citing the letter written by his predecessor to Cardinal Fiorenzo Angelini in 1992 for the institution of the Day.

There are many patients in the hospitals, but also many at home, even more alone. I hope that they will be visited frequently, so that they do not feel excluded from the community, and that they may experience, through the closeness of those whom they encounter, the presence of Christ Who passes today in the midst of those ailing in body and spirit. Unfortunately, the worst discrimination suffered by the poor—and the sick are poor in health—is the lack of spiritual attention. They need God and we must not fail to offer them His friendship, His blessing, His Word, the celebration of the Sacraments and a journey of growth and maturity in the faith (see *Evanglii Gaudium*, no. 200).

Speech, February 10, 2017

Valuable Members of the Church

The sick are valuable members of the Church . . . By the grace of God and the intercession of Mary, Health of the Sick, may they become strong in weakness, and "receive the grace to fill up what is lacking in the sufferings of Christ for His body, the Church. For that body, in the image of the risen Lord's own, keeps its wounds, the marks of a hard struggle, but they are wounds transfigured for ever by love" (Homily for the Jubilee for the Sick and Persons with Disabilities, June 12, 2016).

Speech, February 10, 2017

The Cross of Illness Is a Seed of Life

Illness is a cross—you know this—but the Cross is always a seed of life, and by bearing it well one can give much life to many people whom we do not know; and then, in Heaven, we will know them.

Homily, *March 12, 2017 (Meeting with the Sick and the Elderly)*

The Duty to Visit Sick People

I ask you, please, in the name of Christ and the Church, to always be merciful; do not encumber the faithful, nor yourselves, with unbearable burdens. For this Jesus reproached the doctors of the law and called them hypocrites. With holy oil you will relieve and console the sick. One of the tasks—perhaps the most tedious, even painful one—is to visit the sick. Do this. Yes, it is good that the lay faithful and deacons go, but do not neglect to touch the flesh of the suffering Christ in the sick. This sanctifies you; it brings you closer to Christ. You will celebrate the liturgy and offer thanks and praise to God throughout the day, praying not only for the people of God but for the whole world.

Homily, Ordination to the Priesthood Mass, May 7, 2017

Silent Presence, Daily Offering, Patient and Joyful Acceptance

Your silent presence, which is more eloquent than a flood of words, your prayers, the daily offering of your sufferings in union with those of Jesus crucified for the salvation of the world, the patient and even joyful acceptance of your condition—all these are a spiritual resource, an asset to every Christian community.

Greeting to the Sick, Conclusion of Holy Mass, Fatima, May 13, 2017

Respect and Love for Those Affected by Huntington's Disease

For far too long the fears and difficulties that characterize the life of people affected by Huntington's Disease have surrounded them with misunderstandings and barriers, veritably excluding them. In many cases the sick and their families have experienced the tragedy of shame, isolation and abandonment. Today, however, we are here because we want to say to ourselves and all the world: "HIDDEN NO MORE!," "OCULTA NUNCA MAS!," "MAI PIU' NASCOSTA!" It is not simply a slogan, so much as a commitment that we all must foster. The strength and conviction with which we pronounce these words derive precisely from what Jesus himself taught us. Throughout his ministry, he met many sick people; he took on their suffering; he tore down the walls of stigma and of marginalization that prevented so many of them from feeling respected and loved.

Speech, May 18, 2017

Disease Does Not Erase Human Dignity

For Jesus, disease is never an obstacle to encountering people, but rather, the contrary. He taught us that the human person is always precious, always endowed with a dignity that nothing and no one can erase, not even disease. Fragility is not an ill. And disease, which is an expression of fragility, cannot and must not make us forget that in the eyes of God our value is always priceless.

Speech, May 18, 2017

Illness as a Moment of Meeting, Sharing, and Solidarity

Disease can also be an opportunity for encounter, for sharing, for solidarity. The sick people who encountered Jesus were restored above all by this awareness. They felt they were listened to, respected, loved. May none of you ever feel you are alone; may none of you feel you are a burden; may no one feel the need to run away. You are precious in the eyes of God; you are precious in the eyes of the Church!

Speech, May 18, 2017

Tools to Help the Sick

Often adding to the disease are poverty, forced separations and a general sense of dismay and mistrust. For this reason, national and international associations and institutions are vital . . . like hands that God uses to sow hope . . . the voices that these people have so as to claim their rights!

Speech, May 18, 2017

A "Solidarity Pact"

There is a great need to spread a culture of life, made up of attitudes and behaviors. A true popular culture, serious, accessible to all, and not based on commercial interests. More specifically, families need to be accompanied on a path of prevention: a path that involves the different generations in a fraternal "pact," a path that values the experience of those who have lived, along with their relatives, the arduous path of oncological pathology.

Speech, June 26, 2017

Every "Periphery" Calls into Question the Responsibility of Every Christian

"Periphery" refers to every man and woman who lives in a condition of marginalization; the periphery is every person confined to the margins of society and relationships, especially when disease infringes upon the usual rhythms of life, as is the case with oncological pathologies. It is the periphery that calls to the responsibility of each one of us, since every Christian, along with every man inspired by the desire for truth and goodness, constitutes a conscious instrument of grace.

Speech, June 26, 2017

"Taking Care" Means Not "Wasting Time"

Caring for others, as witnessed in everyday life with many people who are sick, is an inestimable wealth for society: it reminds the entire civil and ecclesial community not to be afraid of closeness, not to be afraid of tenderness, not to be afraid of "spending time" with bonds that offer and welcome mutual support and comfort, spaces for authentic rather than formal solidarity.

Speech, June 26, 2017

Cancer Prevention Can Be Extended to All

Since health is a primary and fundamental common good for every person, it is to be hoped that oncological prevention be extended to all, thanks to collaboration between public and private services, civil and charitable initiatives. In this way, with your specific contribution, in this sector too we can try to ensure that our societies become ever more inclusive.

Speech, June 26, 2017

CONCLUSION

In light of what Pope Francis has expressed with great mercy and extraordinary humanity, one can fully understand how even the most serious illnesses can be an opportunity for union, sharing, and solidarity.

The Argentinian pope always emphasizes the sacredness of human life by focusing on the importance of the human person who must never lose dignity or respectability and by constantly promoting a culture of encounter and fraternal sharing with the sick person. Human life is always precious in the eyes of the Lord, no matter one's condition of life, and "people immersed in the mystery of suffering and pain, when they accept these in faith, can themselves become living witnesses of a faith capable of embracing suffering, even without being able to understand its full meaning" (Message, December 3, 2014). The social doctrine of the Church, with its integral vision of man as a personal and social being, is a compass for a sure defense of the sick and gives hope and consolation while affirming the true value of suffering.

"The world does not become better because only apparently 'perfect' people live there," warns Pope Francis in his homily from June 12, 2016, "but when human solidarity, mutual acceptance and respect increase." Today, the pope continues, "we are even told that it is better to eliminate [sick or disabled persons] . . . because they become an unacceptable economic burden in time of crisis." Yet while "there is not always a medicine for everything; the answer is always love," the pope says, warning us against "pietism" that keeps people in "enclosures."

Thus, sickness finds its ultimate meaning in Christ, and the proposed solution to the pathology of sadness is to love unconditionally, in spite of everything.

In today's culture, where imperfections must be hidden away and where care for one's body, which has become almost an obsession, is big business, Pope Francis encourages people to think about and understand dynamics that should not be consigned to oblivion.

All too often people shut their eyes in the face of sickness, failing to understand the real meaning of life, as they should.

The pope from Buenos Aires explains the value of a person with this valuable and meaningful warning: "The way we experience illness and disability is an index of the love we are ready to offer. The way we face suffering and limitation is the measure of our freedom to give meaning to life's experiences, even when they strike us as meaningless and unmerited" (Homily June 12, 2016).

Yes, individuals should not be troubled by their sufferings, because they can become strong even in these situations. This is attested to by sick people who have encountered Jesus. This encounter gave them strength and reinvigorated them because they experienced what it means to be accepted, respected, and loved. They did not feel alone.

It is therefore important to work for the growth of a culture of respect for life and health to defend the integrity of persons (like the sick) who should never have to be afraid of being abandoned or neglected.

It is our task "to develop an 'antidote' to this way of considering the elderly, or people with disabilities, almost as if they were lives no longer worth living" (Speech, June 21, 2015). In his speeches, Pope Francis reiterates the inviolability of the life of the person and suggests the way to overcome afflictions and torment. "Suffering is not a value in itself but a reality that Jesus teaches us to live with the right attitude. There are, in fact, right ways and wrong ways to experience pain and suffering. The wrong attitude is experiencing pain passively, letting ourselves be swept up in inertia and giving up. Reacting with rebellion and denial is not the correct attitude either. Jesus teaches us to experience pain by accepting the reality of life with trust and hope and *by putting the love of God and our neighbors too into suffering*: it is love that transforms all things" (Speech, May 17, 2014). Also of fundamental importance is the value of time spent close to the sick, which is seen as taking responsibility for our neighbor to nourish faith in Christ and educate humanity to protect and "administer Creation as a whole, as a gift entrusted to the responsibility of every generation, so that it is handed down as intact and humanly livable as possible to the coming generations" (Speech, November 19, 2015).